WRITING ABOUT SEXUAL ASSAULT

AN INCOMPLETE GUIDE

Salt & Sage Books

SALT & SAGE BOOKS

Cover designed by Blue Water Books

eBook ISBN 978-1-7349234-5-2

Paperback ISBN 978-1-7349234-6-9

To the people healing the world through their creations.

CONTENT WARNING &
STATISTICS

As this book deals with the difficult topic of sexual assault, we encourage you to take the time to be careful with your own mental and emotional health as you read this book. We have done our best to present the information in a way that is easy to understand, but by its very nature, there are several discussions in this book that are quite painful.

Take your time reading. Take breaks between sections if you feel yourself becoming overwhelmed. Talk with trusted friends and family if the information and insights shared are hard for you to process. The more compassionate you are with yourself, the more compassionately you'll be able to write these characters and their traumatic experiences.

As you read, you may realize that you have been a victim of sexual assault. You may realize that you have perpetuated sexual assault. These realizations are both critical and difficult to come to grips with. If you need someone to talk to, we highly recommend RAINN's sexual assault telephone hotline: 1.800.656.HOPE (4673). We also encourage you to seek out the help of a qualified therapist.[1]

Statistics

Statistics provided reflect available information in the United States of America. We recognize that these statistics are exclusionary by nature, and encourage you to take a look at worldwide statistics to get a broader picture, particularly if your story is not set in the United States.

---

1. https://www.rainn.org/articles/how-can-therapy-help

Dear Reader:

Stories are a serious magic, with the power to speak truth and healing, and to help those with hidden wounds feel seen.

So many of us share a story about being violated by perpetrators. Some people's stories go on to include related losses as well—our sense of safety, our health. Too many of us have assault stories with sequels that read "and they were never able to go home or be with their people again."

Please, listen and learn. We who wrote this want so much to help you understand the multiple ways sexual assault causes pain. We share our experiences in the hope of helping you get this right, so that you and your stories may be another truth-telling place of refuge for those who need it most.

But you, dear reader, you have the power to help change that. By listening to our lived experiences, you can tell stories that will better honor the wounds so many of us carry.

To make people feel seen, and known, and less alone: this is the loving magic authors can wield.

May you seriously work your story magic for good,

Sachiko Burton

Dear Reader,

Thank you so much for purchasing this guide. I am incredibly happy that people like you are making a point to write accurate, well-rounded characters, and I applaud your willingness to learn and listen. That being said, this guide is incomplete. Sexual assault comes in too many forms, and everyone's experience is different.

After reading this guide, I urge you to dive deeper into the sources listed within it for a more in-depth understanding and to reach out to people who are willing to speak with you to gain a diverse perspective. Our sensitivity readers are always available for any additional questions you may have.

Above all, one of the most healing things for me was the process of dispelling shame, so I thank you for giving me the opportunity to speak about aspects of my life that most people deem unspeakable. Readers like you are taking one more step toward the destigmatization sexual assault survivors so desperately need. So, thank you for helping me. I hope this helps you enrich your understanding of what sexual assault is, how people react to it, and how to portray it in a way that is not only accurate but helpful.

Wishing you the best of luck on your journey in writing and life,

Katherine DeGilio

Dear Reader,

I volunteered to help write this guide because I want to help authors depict rape and sexual assault sensitively and with a better understanding of the issues surrounding it. I am a survivor myself—as all who have contributed to this guide are—and I want to help authors avoid causing unintentional harm.

I want fiction to be able to represent the immense diversity of human relationships accurately and with all their nuances. For this to happen, it is vital for authors to know what rape and sexual assault really are, what they can look like, and what impact they can have.

Thank you for being here to learn more about it.

An Anonymous Contributor

Dear Reader,

It is reassuring to know that you are interested in representing victims of rape and sexual assault in an understanding and compassionate manner. All too often, fictional depictions of rape come across as victim-blaming, shaming, or callous.

I know and understand the research you are doing is mentally draining and maybe even a little scary to process. I hope the information we've shared in this guide is helpful as you tackle this subject.

Best wishes,

Lee Anne

WHY THIS BOOK?

Dear Reader,

Welcome to *How to Write About Sexual Assault*, part of Salt & Sage Books' Incomplete Guide series. We're glad to have you here!

Do you remember the first time you read a book and thought, "Ah! That's me!"? That ringing inside of being seen?

I do. As a child, I was obsessed with a Cinderella book my Grandma had given me. Cinderella was white, blond, and female, just like me. I was probably two.

When we started doing interviews for Salt & Sage, we asked, "When have you felt seen?" The answers we've heard from our incredible editors & readers have been inspiring and heartbreaking. Some of them have been avid readers their whole lives, but have yet to read about someone who looks like them, feels like them, talks like them. Some of them shared instances where they hadn't been seen, and even more shared stories of how what they read, watched, or heard was actively harmful to them.

Fast forward to 2019. Salt & Sage Books was born basically overnight out of a feeling of urgency about my own freelance editing career and the careers of my editor friends. It rapidly grew from there, and one of Salt & Sage's most popular services is a sensitivity read. I'm really proud of the sensitivity reading services we provide. We've worked hard to create an inclusive, diverse, and safe place for our readers and editors to thrive. Salt & Sage is all about quality editing with kindness—and kindness isn't just an encouraging edit letter or complimentary in-line notes. Kindness is helping authors like you (like me!) who want to do better and be better, but aren't sure where to start. That meant providing a level of sensitivity reading beyond a basic rubber stamp of yes/no.

As I read through the sensitivity reader letters, I noticed a pattern: the same concerns were appearing again and again in the letters from our Black readers. I saw the same pattern from our trans readers. Once I noticed it, the pattern showed up everywhere: our sensitivity readers were regularly rehashing the same concerns related to their identities.

This got me thinking—if our authors were consistently having the same issues, could we help in a more targeted way? And what about the authors for whom a sensitivity read is too expensive?

The more I thought about it, the more I liked the idea. I've talked to lots of people in the writing world about writing diversely, and the same thing stops nearly all of them: fear. They don't know where to start. They aren't sure that their Googled information is accurate. They don't know anyone who they can ask, or they are too nervous to ask.

After lots of brainstorming about the best way to provide this information, the Incomplete Guides were born. You're currently reading our Incomplete Guide about how to write sexual assault. This was written entirely by our editors who have experienced sexual assault. They've addressed the most common areas of concern that pop up in their sensitivity reading. You'll see sections where they write from their own point of view. Multiple authors have contributed to each section. Some of them have included their names; others have chosen to remain anonymous for their own safety. (Doxxing is still a very real concern, and one we actively try to protect our editors against.)

Of course, even though this was written and edited by multiple editors and sensitivity readers who have experienced sexual assault, we called the guide *incomplete* for a reason—it's not a blank check, nor is it a rubber stamp. Even if you address everything in this guide, you should still seek input from at least one person who has experienced the same level and type of sexual assault as your character. Salt & Sage Books has sensitivity readers on staff, but many creatives also have success posting about their specific needs on Twitter's writing hashtags. Be sure to pay your readers for their labor. Listen carefully to their feedback, and you will most certainly write a better story.

We hope that *How to Write About Sexual Assault: An Incomplete Guide* will be a helpful resource as you write about this difficult and common occurrence. We invite you to step inside the viewpoint of our editors and sensitivity readers experience a deeper, more impactful form of researching. We hope that will help you confront your own biases when writing characters who have experienced sexual assault.

As we discuss in Chapter 6, "Making careful, honoring choices in [your story] can make the difference between a story that validates trauma, and a story that reenacts it."

We hope that you will continue to create thoughtful, nuanced characters, and worlds that reflect the reality of sexual assault and its consequences. We hope that you will be part of the movement to create more diverse books and other creative content. It's critical work. It's occasionally difficult. It's deeply worth the effort.

May you write books that help people feel seen.

Yours,

Erin Olds

she/her

CEO, Salt & Sage Books

SEXUAL ASSAULT IS EXTREMELY COMMON

As the title to this chapter suggests, sexual assault is extremely common. However, here we run into the limiting fact that *reported* sexual assaults are common. This necessarily indicates that unreported sexual assaults are actually far more common than the collected data suggests. See Chapter 5 for more discussion about why people do (and don't) report sexual assaults.

Let's look at the data that we do have, bearing in mind that these statistics are incomplete at best. To give a broad overview, we'll look at definitions, then at the *what, who, whom, when, and where* of sexual assault.

SEXUAL ASSAULT

Sexual assault is any sexual contact or behavior that occurs without the explicit consent of the victim.

- Some forms of sexual assault include:
- Fondling or unwanted sexual touching
- Forcing a victim to perform sexual acts, such as oral sex or penetrating the perpetrator's body
- Attempted rape
- Penetration of the victim's body, i.e., rape

Rape is a form of sexual assault, but not all sexual assault is rape. Rape may be defined differently in different places, but the general definition includes unlawful, nonconsensual sexual intercourse or sexual penetration of a person's vagina, anus, or mouth by a perpetrator's sex organ, body part, or foreign object.

FORCE

Force doesn't always refer to physical pressure. Perpetrators may use emotional coercion, psychological force, or manipulation to coerce a victim into nonconsensual sex. Some perpetrators will use threats to force a victim to comply, such as threatening to hurt the victim or their family or other intimidation tactics.

Force may also be known as "duress."

Consent

Consent is the active, ongoing, and freely given agreement a person gives to engage in sexual activity with another person.

Sexual assault can take many different forms, but one thing always remains the same:

It's never the victim's fault.

From a legal standpoint, sexual assault is "any nonconsensual sexual act proscribed by Federal, tribal, or State law, including when the victim lacks capacity to consent."[1]

Our culture has commonly described sexual assault as a crime of passion, affection, or attraction, and this can contribute to the inaccurate view that if the person who assaulted another did so while feeling attracted to them, while expressing affection or feeling love, that it isn't bad or isn't really assault. These conditions can exist, and yet what has happened is still assault.

Sexual contact without consent is sexual assault or rape.

Rape is sexual activity or sexual intercourse carried out forcibly or under threat of injury against a person's will, or with a person who is beneath a certain age or incapable of valid consent because of mental limitations, intoxication, unconsciousness, or deception.

WHAT IS CONSENT?

Consent is a clear "yes" to sexual activity.

There are some cases where a person can't legally give consent. For instance, if someone is under the age of legal consent, if they are not mentally able (due to disability or illness), if they're not physically able (asleep, passed out, drugged, drunk, or high), or if they are threatened, manipulated, coerced, or forced into agreeing.

An absence of a "no" does not mean "yes." Consent must be active to truly be consent.

If someone said "yes" in the past, that does not mean that they are saying "yes" presently. Consent must be part of every sexual activity.

Consent is not unlimited. Someone may consent to kissing, for example, but that doesn't give consent for someone to remove clothing.

Being in a relationship doesn't mean that consent is automatic.

If a person does not fight back, that does not mean there is consent. Wearing sexy clothing, flirting, and dancing do not equal consent for sexual activity. [2]

TROPES AROUND CONSENT

One common trope related to consent is "Lie Back and Think of England." In this trope, sex is a chore or a duty. While frequently played for laughs, this trope is, at its core, about the lack of consent. If sex is something to be endured, it is by definition nonconsensual. That said, of course someone can consent to sex but still not enjoy it.[3]

One impact of this poor definition of consent is the idea that marital rape does not exist.

According to one study, "Approximately 10-14% of married women are raped by their husbands in the United States."[4] Legally, this has only recently been rectified.

> Rape—any nonconsensual sexual intercourse—between non-spouses has always been illegal. However, until 1975, every state had a "marital exemption" that allowed a husband to rape his wife without fear of legal consequences.... Since 1993, all 50 states and DC have enacted laws against marital rape.[5]

Marital rape is just as serious as other forms of sexual violence, and should be treated as such. In addition, living with one's assaulter adds an extra layer of intensity to an immensely difficult situation.

As you write characters who are in complex relationships, it is important to remember that force can be exerted in subtle ways. For example, intimate touching to evoke arousal despite the spouse expressing disinterest, verbally pointing out things the spouse has done for their partner recently, or expressing that they "had a hard day" or "need to get their mind off of [upsetting event]." These examples of manipulative behavior can be extremely subtle, but their subtle nature does not change the fact that force is being applied to push someone into sexual behavior.

It's a common misconception that sexual assault has to be violent for it to be assault, but it is *regularly not violent*. Sexual assault can happen quietly. That doesn't make it any less of an assault. The coercion of sexual assault may not be due to a deadly weapon, but rather to another kind of coercion, like emotional abuse—and this kind of coercion can even happen silently.[678]

In addition, the impact of shock and survival instincts cannot be discounted: fight, flight, freeze, and fawn are instinctual reactions to conflict. Fight, flight, and freeze are fairly well known. Fight is aggression; flight is fleeing or running; and freeze misbecoming incapable of making a choice or even moving.

  The fawn response involves immediately moving to try to please a person to avoid any conflict. This is often a response developed in childhood trauma, where a parent or a significant authority figure is the abuser. Children go into a fawn-like response to attempt to avoid the abuse, which may be verbal, physical, or sexual, by being a pleaser. In other words, they preemptively attempt to appease the abuser by agreeing, answering what they know the parent wants to hear, or by ignoring their personal feelings and desires and do anything and everything to prevent the abuse. [9]

WHERE DOES SEXUAL ASSAULT HAPPEN?

It's commonly believed that rape mostly happens in the back alleys of the bad part of town, public restrooms, or at college frat parties. People often comfort themselves with the belief that rape and assault are what happen in other countries, other communities, other families, but not at home.

But sexual assault can affect anyone of any age, nationality, race, religion, or gender, and is usually a crime of acquaintance. Perpetrators sexually assault people in homes, schools, hospitals, stores, and churches-—basically, anywhere humans usually are. Sexual assault literally happens where we live.

WHO PERPETRATES SEXUAL ASSAULT?

The vast majority of rapes and sexual assaults perpetrators commit are upon people the perpetrators know. This contradicts the common misconception of the majority of rapes and assaults being committed by strangers.

According to RAINN, eight out of ten rapes are committed by someone known by the victim.

The statistics are even starker for cases of child rape: 93% of those who rape or sexually assault a child are either that child's family member, or someone else the child knows.

This is a very important consideration. We often talk about the statistical frequency of suffering sexual assault and rape, but we don't often discuss the corollary: that each of these crimes were committed by someone, someone who (according to statistics) has likely never been charged with a crime or served a sentence. It means there are many people in our communities who have raped or assaulted someone without being held accountable.

Who is Assaulted?

It is estimated that an American is sexually assaulted every 73 seconds. On average, there are 433,648 victims (age twelve or older) of rape and sexual assault each year in the United States.[10]

Those found to be most at risk of sexual violence such as rape are people in the age range of twelve to thirty-four, but people of any age, sex, gender, ethnicity, race, ability, etc. can be victims of sexual assault.[11]

One out of every six American women has been the victim of an attempted or completed rape; however, sexual assault is not gendered. It can be perpetrated against men by women, man to man, woman to woman, and nonbinary people to nonbinary people.

Unsurprisingly, people in vulnerable populations (people with less access to financial or social resources) who are more vulnerable to crime are also at greater risk for sexual assault and rape. Transgender, genderqueer, and gender nonconforming people are more likely to be sexually assaulted than cisgendered people.

According to RAINN, "21% of TGQN (transgender, genderqueer, nonconforming) college students have been sexually assaulted, compared to 18% of the non-TGQN females, and 4% of the non-TGQN males."[12] This number is likely much higher as, due to trauma, members of marginalized communities have cause to be less trusting of authority figures and as a result, are sometimes less likely to report.

The common perception of rape and sexual assault is that men perpetrate it against women. While that does constitute the majority of reported cases of sexual assault, it's important to keep in mind that sexual assault is the most underreported crime, and that some forms of sexual assault—especially against men—are even more underreported than male-on-female sexual violence. Again, it is critical to emphasize that these are merely the reported statistics. There is every indication that the actual numbers are much higher.

MEDICAL SEXUAL ASSAULT

Medical sexual assault is often viewed only as outright rape or sexual advances or inappropriate sexual touching during exams by medical professionals. However, medical sexual assault also occurs when a medical professional touches or performs a procedure on a person's breasts, buttocks, pubic area, external genitals, inside the urethra (such as placing a catheter), or anally or vaginally without asking for consent.

For example, one of our editors was in the hospital for a childbirth induction, and during a vaginal exam, the female obstetrician did an extremely painful procedure without warning or consent, causing the patient a great deal of shock, pain, and emotional trauma. Another incident happened after the birth, when a male obstetrician sewed up the patient's vaginal tear after childbirth, turned to the patient's spouse, and said, "There. I put in an extra stitch to tighten things up for you." He did this without her consent. Both of these incidences constitute medical sexual assault.

Here are just a few things to be made aware of when writing medical scenes:

 It's okay for the examiner to:

Explain each part of the exam to you before and while it is happening.

Use gloves.

Encourage you to tell them if something feels wrong or uncomfortable.

Is the same sex as you, if you have asked.

Only ask you to undress the part of your body being examined.

It's NOT okay for the examiner to:

Refuse to answer your questions or tell you to be quiet.

Examine private parts without gloves.

Refuse to tell you what they are doing or why they are doing it.

Decline to have another person in the room with you.

Insist that you undress parts of your body they are not examining.

Ask you questions about your sexual activity that make you uncomfortable.[13]

For more on what constitutes medical sexual assault, and to find out what you can do to get help if you realize you've been medically sexually assaulted, please see RAINN's website.

GIVEN that sexual assault and rape are so commonly experienced, it's important that when you create storylines around this, you take your audience into consideration. There is some controversy around content warnings, but they are a way to show your audience that you care about their mental and emotional health. If your piece includes a scene of sexual assault, we would encourage you to put a content warning on it.

RAPE IS so common and so commonly misunderstood that it's possible that you, our reader, may now be seeing past experiences in a new light..

You may have just realized that what happened was assault.

If this is you, you are not alone. Please reach out to RAINN's help line: 1.800.656.HOPE (4673).

We said it at the beginning of the chapter, and will repeat it throughout the Guide, but if you were sexually assaulted, it is not your fault—no matter the circumstances.

If your character is sexually assaulted, it is not their fault, regardless of the circumstances.

It is *never the victim's fault.*

---

1. https://www.justice.gov/ovw/sexual-assault
2. https://www.womenshealth.gov/relationships-and-safety/sexual-assault-and-rape/sexual-assault
3. https://tvtropes.org/pmwiki/pmwiki.php/Main/LieBackAndThinkOfEngland
4. https://vawnet.org/material/marital-rape-new-research-and-directions
5. https://www.criminaldefenselawyer.com/marital-rape-laws.html
6. https://www.psychologytoday.com/us/blog/making-sense-chaos/202005/the-bizarre-legal-loopholes-surrounding-spousal-rape
7. https://time.com/3976180/marital-rape/
8. https://psychcentral.com/lib/marital-rape/
9. https://www.psychologytoday.com/us/blog/addiction-and-recovery/202008/understanding-fight-flight-freeze-and-the-fawn-response
10. https://www.rainn.org/statistics/victims-sexual-violence
11. https://www.rainn.org/statistics/victims-sexual-violence
12. https://www.rainn.org/statistics/campus-sexual-violence
13. https://www.rainn.org/articles/sexual-abuse-medical-professionals

2

IT WAS PROBABLY SOMEONE WE KNEW

The most common depiction of rape and/or sexual assault in media tends to be along the lines of stranger danger. Usually, someone (generally a young woman) is randomly attacked by a villainous man while minding her own business, is the victim of a robbery or mugging that then escalates, or has a one-night stand with somebody who then turns violent.

All of these scenarios can and do happen. However, they are statistically not the most likely version of events. RAINN (the Rape, Abuse & Incest National Network) found that roughly 80% of rapes involve somebody that the victim knows.[1] This is a trend that is also reflected in the UK—Rape Crisis England & Wales found that "approximately 90% of those who are raped know the perpetrator prior to the offence."[2]

There is a popular perception among the general public that strangers are the people most likely to attack them. They then take measures to prevent such attacks, rather than being aware of red flags in the people they see every day: colleagues, friends, friends-of-friends, relatives, or even their own partners. Because they do not expect these people to attack them—since there is a common belief that it is always an obviously villainous stranger who does such things—they may miss warning signs.

Having said that, it is important to immediately clarify that *the victim is not responsible for stopping their own rape.* This would require not just a state of constant vigilance and paranoia, which is horrendously unfair to expect from anyone, but literal mind reading, flawless self-defense techniques, and a ton of sheer good luck. It is a ludicrous and cruel thing to tell somebody that they could have prevented what happened to them, as if they should have "known better" somehow.

The fault for rape and sexual assault *always* lies with the perpetrator. If someone tells you they've been stabbed, your response shouldn't be that they should have been wearing armor.

Creating one dominant image of what a rapist looks like can be harmful to the public understanding of what rape is and who commits it. The idea that rape is something that always involves a drugging and/or beating by a stranger means that when somebody comes forward about being raped by their partner, they are less likely to be believed. Their experience is not what society thinks rape looks like.

When most people think of a rapist, they are more likely to think of something like the assailants from *Last House on the Left* or *I Spit On Your Grave*: a clearly suspicious-looking person (or people) who behaves in a threatening way from the first interaction before combining their sexual assault with a level of physical violence that almost kills the victim. This is what is seen as "real" rape, and this is why scenes such as the one between Rachael and Deckard from *Blade Runner* often do not register as assault.

Here is a detailed breakdown of what happens in that particular scene.[3] That this scene contains descriptions of sexual assault that may be triggering to some readers.

Deckard (the protagonist) kisses Rachael on the cheek. She pulls back and looks at him, and then backs away when he tries to kiss her again. She then tries to leave the room. Deckard follows her. When she tries to open the door, he slams it shut again with a closed fist before invading her personal space again. He grabs her by the arms and shoves her quite heavily against the window. He approaches again with his hands out, about to touch her face, and again she flinches away. He puts his hands on her shoulders and shoves her again, though not as heavily this time. Rachael clearly appears distressed and close to tears. Deckard then kisses her on the mouth, and she begins to sob.

Deckard says: "Kiss me."

Rachael begins to say what sounds like: "I can't rely on myself," but Deckard interrupts with "Say 'kiss me.'"

Rachael says: "Kiss me."

She continues to cry while he kisses her.

Then Deckard says: "I want you."

Rachael repeats after him: "I want you."

Deckard says: "Again."

Rachael says: "I want you," and then "Put your hands on me."

Deckard kisses her again, and the film cuts to the next day, leaving the audience to assume they had sex.

If this scene happened in real life, it would undoubtedly be assault: Rachael has backed away but been followed, tried to leave and been stopped, been literally pushed against a window so that she can't get away, is in tears, and is then forced to say that she wants whatever comes next. It is important to note that these two people are not strangers: they have met several times previously, and Rachael is currently staying at Deckard's apartment.

This removal of choice—particularly the blocking of the door and the clear physical threat that the other person can and will over-power her—makes whatever happens afterwards what should be an obvious example of assault and/or rape. If any person does not feel that they can say no, or have said no (verbally or physically) and then had their wishes ignored, they cannot give consent.

But because most media depicts rape and assault as something that always involves screaming, weapons, blood, restraints, and so on, it can be hard for survivors to realize that this is what has happened to them. In the same way, many rapists don't think that what they did was "really" rape—though they may admit to having "coerced somebody to intercourse by holding them down" and similar phrasings.[4] They believe that if they didn't cause bruises, it can't have been rape. This is a large part of rape culture (more in Chapter 3).

As you consider including scenes of rape and sexual assault in your manuscript, think carefully and deeply. The descriptions that you use can and will contribute to the readers' idea of what rape is, and what rapists are like. Showing that a rapist can be a husband or a friend, not just a stranger, is an important step towards discussing those far more common attacks.

---

1. https://www.rainn.org/statistics/perpetrators-sexual-violence
2. https://rapecrisis.org.uk/get-informed/about-sexual-violence/statistics-sexual-violence/
3. You can watch it for yourself here: https://www.youtube.com/watch?v=pOfvq5ZO-Qw

   There is also an interesting video by Pop Culture Detective that goes into more depth about other scenes with Harrison Ford here: https://www.youtube.com/watch?v=wWoP8VpbpYI
4. https://www.liebertpub.com/doi/pdf/10.1089/vio.2014.0022

RAPE CULTURE

R ape culture is a social environment in which media and popular culture normalize and excuse sexual violence.

Rape culture redefines rape.

Another way rape culture's broad denial of rape manifests is through a narrow redefinition of sexual assault.

What this looks like is people or institutions redefining sexual assault only as an attack that involves a deadly weapon where a victim must choose to be assaulted to survive. Some people narrow that definition even further—to require that victims must prove that they nearly died trying to stop their attacker. These definitions exclude multiple forms of sexual assault, which can involve emotional or situational coercion.

Force doesn't have to be physical force; it can be emotional or financial coercion. It can be threats to withhold sleep from the victim, threats to harm the victim's loved ones, and/or threats to remove financial or professional support, and threats to withdraw affection.

The key to understanding what defines sexual assault is understanding what constitutes "duress" and "consent."

Duress: threats, violence, constraints, or other action brought to bear on someone to do something against their will or better judgment.

Consent: Active and ongoing agreement to be sexual with someone.

Rape culture may seek to redefine sexual assault by challenging or limiting the definitions of duress or consent.

Why? Because if you can narrow the definition of what constitutes sexual assault, then you can use words to make a problem disappear. That's a key part of denial.

Rape culture makes rape seem normal or fun.

Rape culture normalizes and trivializes assault. Commonly used phrases include "Boys will be boys," "It's just a locker room thing," or "That's what happens at parties."

That means everyone—victims, perpetrators, support people, the justice system—may struggle to define assault, and that struggle makes it more difficult for assault victims to recognize what's been done to them, which discourages reporting.

The same struggle may also enable perpetrators in excusing or denying how they've assaulted others. This can look and sound like "We all did that at that party," or "It's just how things were back then."

Part of this cultural denial is the refusal to acknowledge that sexual assault happens in a given culture. One way people convey this denial is by saying, "Oh, that doesn't happen *here*. That happens only in other places where they have lower standards or worse people." Refusing to accept that sexual assault is perpetrated everywhere can motivate people to seek to normalize assault in order to maintain a false sense of safety, or a sense of cultural superiority.

Rape culture seeks to control through fear.

Rape culture is also perpetuated through targeted fear. Sexual assault is perpetrated by anyone upon anyone, but the majority of reported assaults are perpetrated by men upon women and girls.

The rape-culture response to this is to expect womxn and girls to live in fear of rape, and to change how they dress, act, and move through their lives in order to try to avoid being raped.

But rape culture doesn't ask the same sacrifices of men.

Rape culture shifts the blame.

By not supporting society through a clear definition of sexual assault, and by expecting potential assault victims to go to extraordinary lengths to try to prevent rape, rape culture blames the victim for failing to control the choices and actions of others. Rape culture will tell the victim that the sexual assault was somehow the victim's fault, that they "asked for it."

Sexual assault and rape are unwanted sexual contact; therefore, by definition, nobody can ask for it. But all too often, people who have been sexually assaulted are treated as though they deserved to be harmed.

Rape culture harms sexual assault victims.

The first harm is in how victims—freshly shattered by their assault—may often internalize the harmful and shaming messages they've absorbed from the rape culture around them, and blame themselves.

This self-blame frequently discourages victims from reporting the assault and seeking needed medical care and legal support (more in Chapter 5).

When victims of assault do report, rape culture may seep in and affect the reporting process. Disclosing assault requires a victim to relive their trauma on a significant level, and rape culture often denies these very vulnerable people the support they need.

Victim-blaming isn't always vicious or callous. It's not always a shouting voice and pointing finger. It can be done subtly, in a soft voice. It can be done even with the best of intentions.

The false belief that the victim is to blame for the crime another committed against them is such a pernicious false belief that police and social workers often take classes in how to best support victims through the reporting process because it's unfortunately common that victims who report sexual assault end up being criminalized.

Rape culture also makes it easier for perpetrators to get away with their crimes. It's very rare for a sexual assault to be reported, and even rarer for a rape case to go to court, but once there, rape-culture narratives are often what the accused's defense attorneys rely on to exonerate the perpetrator.

* * *

WHAT DOES RAPE CULTURE SOUND LIKE?

Some examples of blaming statements are:

- "You gave the wrong signals or mixed signals."
- "Don't dress like a slut."
- "You were asking for it."
- "Boys will be boys."
- "Are you sure you were raped?"
- "They didn't mean it like that."
- "How could you let that happen?"
- "You shouldn't've been out at night."

- "You should've taken a self-defense class."
- "Why didn't you have a gun?"
- "Didn't you tell them to stop?"
- "Now you're ruined."
- "It would be better to die than to let someone take your virtue."[1]

All of these statements can be intensely harmful to someone who has been assaulted. Part of the way abusers work is by convincing victims that they're dumb, stupid, or worthless. When people tell those who've been assaulted that they might've escaped if they'd just been smarter or stronger or better, then they're echoing the abusers and confirming their lies as truth. Don't ever do this to someone already so vulnerable.

***

How to Responsibly Approach Rape Culture as a Writer

When you write about sexual assault, you become a witness to a crime. Even though that crime may be fictional, it still feels real to those reading it, and even more so for those who've had to live through it. The last thing a sexual assault victim needs is a story that only reinforces the harmful false beliefs promulgated by rape culture.

Writing a story that shows a sexual assault victim experiencing a lack of support or even being blamed or mistreated is not always, in itself, harmful.[2]

What *is* harmful is when you as the writer (and again, as primary witness to the fictional assault) fail to testify on behalf of the victim in your story.

Yes, acknowledge and even portray the common, harmful effects of rape culture. But please also counter that with the healing truth: that nobody asks to be assaulted, and nobody deserves it.

Whether through your narration or the words and actions of other characters in the story, your story can say, "Yes, emotional coercion is also sexual assault." Your story can say, "It was not your fault, and you did not deserve it."[3]

Ideally, when you write about sexual assault, try to write in such a way that those who've had to suffer it feel seen and heard, and that those who haven't can walk away from your words learning how to better support those who have.

———————

1. https://www.cosmopolitan.com/uk/reports/a31377/everyday-sexism-language/
2. https://www.abc.net.au/news/2020-01-29/sexual-assault-legal-system-horror-show-for-survivors/11903584
3. https://thetruthaboutrapeculture.wordpress.com/2013/11/21/no-one-is-asking-for-it/

4

CONSENSUAL SEX CAN TURN INTO ASSAULT

One of the most important things to understand about sexual consent is that it is an ongoing process, and therefore it can change depending on what is happening and how the people involved are feeling.

For example: A person asks their partner if they want to have penetrative sex, and their partner agrees. Halfway through, the partner begins to experience pain, and asks to stop. If the person does not stop, they are now assaulting their partner, even though their partner initially agreed.

The idea that consent can be revoked in the middle of a sex act is one that receives a lot of pushback, because the general view in society is that once a person—particularly a woman—has given consent, she is then obligated to continue. For example, a 2018 YouGov study showed that a third of men believed that a woman couldn't change her mind after sex had started.[1] In North Carolina, continued sex after one partner revoked consent was not considered a crime until 2019.[2]

An example of consensual sex becoming assault is the initial sex scene from *Gerald's Game*[3], where Jessie agrees to experiment with BDSM with her husband, Gerald. She consents to him hand-cuffing her to the bed. However, he then initiates roleplay of a rape fantasy, which she did not know about or consent to. She says that she doesn't like it and asks him repeatedly to stop, which he eventually does—but he then attempts to reinitiate sex, and she has to bite him to get him to back off. If he had gone through with his second attempt, it would undoubtedly have been rape, and his other behaviors absolutely qualify as sexual assault.

So, though the scene started with Jessie consensually trying something new for her partner, he initiated a different activity that had not been discussed and did not stop when asked—turning it into assault.

The key things here are:

1. Gerald was not truthful about what he wanted, and so Jessie could not consent to it.
2. Gerald did not immediately stop when asked.
3. Gerald attempted to initiate sex again despite Jessie clearly not being comfortable with it and repeatedly asking him to take the handcuffs off her.

This is a good demonstration of how someone can revoke consent once they realize they are not enjoying themselves, and an equally good demonstration of how their partner might attempt to ignore that revocation.

If you are writing a sex scene where you want to show healthy consent and positive sexual dynamics, you may want to consider what everybody has consented to and at which points that consent may need to be reaffirmed. These points may include trying something new or unusual for that couple, or moving from one kind of sex to another.

It is incredibly important to know the difference between rape/sexual assault and complicated/unhealthy sexual dynamics. This is for two reasons:

First, a lot of scenes that actually depict rape (e.g. showing a use of force that has not been consented to) are presented in fiction as just "intense sex," which contributes to the rape culture in our society.[4]

Second, authors should be able to show relationships where people are bad for each other without accidentally or deliberately relying on rape or sexual assault to communicate that dynamic.

There's a prevailing view that asking for consent isn't "sexy," which may be an issue if what you are trying to do is write a sexy scene. However, there are lots of ways to have your characters check in on their partner to make sure they're enjoying themselves.

You might consider using verbal consent, such as:

- "Do you like that?"
- "Tell me what you want."
- "Does that feel good?"
- "Do you want this?"
- "Do you want more?"

And other variations on this theme, answered with some form of an enthusiastic yes. Obviously, a huge part of sex is also body language and nonverbal consent, so consider using that as well—for example:

- He pulled him closer.
- She arched into his touch.
- They kissed back, hard.
- She guided her hand lower.
- She wrapped her arms around them.

Another thing to be mindful of is making sure that all the parties involved are clearly giving consent—for example, in heterosexual sex scenes, there's often an unconscious assumption that the man is "in charge" and it's only the woman who needs to give consent, because there is a societal assumption that men always want sex. But the man needs to be shown to be fully into it as well. Make sure that everyone involved in the sex is clearly enjoying themselves.

This is advice intended for where you are trying to show healthy, positive sex scenes. This way, you can avoid accidentally writing something that reads as assault when it was intended to be consensual.

Having said this, there is also a place in fiction for exploring unhealthy and complex sex between partners that does not involve rape and assault. For example, you may want to show somebody who is uncertain about what they want, but wants to explore themselves and their sexuality with their partner. This might include them not knowing if they'll enjoy something, but still consenting to it because they want to know what it feels like or want to try it for their partner.

Another example might be if you want to show "angry sex": consensual sex which happens because the people involved are angry with each other and are expressing themselves physically rather than verbally. This is often an incredibly unhealthy way to try to resolve conflict, but the sex itself can still be consensual. A sexual dynamic can be destructive without being assault. An existing example of this is Buffy and Spike's first sex scene from *Buffy the Vampire Slayer*.[5]

These examples show that "unhealthy/destructive sex" can be completely separate to "consensual sex that becomes assault"—though obviously, assault is inherently destructive. However, it is important to draw a distinction between complicated and/or unhealthy sex, and sexual assault. This distinction is consent.

———————————

1. https://yougov.co.uk/topics/resources/articles-reports/2018/12/01/publics-attitudes-sexual-consent
2. https://www.newsobserver.com/news/politics-government/article237155589.html
3. Specifically the film, as this writer has not read the book. See the perspective of another author in Chapter 10.
4. https://rpe.co.nz/what-is-rape-culture/
5. https://www.youtube.com/watch?v=sjruixPe0f8

UNDERREPORTING: THE REASONS

Sexual assault is a serious crime, and the benefits of reporting sexual assault may seem clear: ideally, the victim empowers themselves by speaking the truth and their timely report can provide information to law enforcement, so that the justice system can prosecute and perhaps protect other current victims (and prevent future victims). Additionally, swiftly reporting sexual assault may mean that the victim can get needed medical attention, legal services, and mental health support through recovery. The victim can heal, and justice can be done.

It sounds great, doesn't it? Unfortunately, it's rarely that simple.

The numbers vary by study, but they all agree that sexual assault is seriously underreported. The vast majority of rapes committed against adult women are not reported, reporting rates for assaults on children are lower, and for sexual assault on men the numbers are even lower still.

To understand why many people don't report their assaults, let's talk about who's affected by sexual assault, how, and why.

***

WHO IS AFFECTED

Sexual assault is traumatic, and often is a profound violation of self, leaving its victims feeling afraid, helpless, and out of control. They may be shocked or dazed, and it's common that they may not immediately remember all the details of the assault—and part of making a report and being believed is remembering the details.

Some people develop post-traumatic stress disorder, which can include flashbacks that make a person feel like they're being assaulted all over again; sometimes memories are so traumatic that people have trouble remembering them clearly at all.

Many victims of sexual assault feel ashamed of being assaulted, or even blame themselves for it. They may experience self-blame, depression, anxiety, and may have a difficult time trusting people. Sexual violence creates a lasting emotional impact. Some people say being assaulted changed the whole course of their life.

When our brain experiences trauma, it will often try to protect us from ever having something so terrible happen to us again. To our brain, talking about an attack in detail is nearly the same thing as experiencing it again, and so our brain will seek to help us avoid that however possible: either by shouting fear at the victim or by trying to help them regain a sense of control through self-blame.

Sometimes trauma even results in some memory loss, which is what happens when the brain decides that memories are so harmful that they simply should never be accessed. Sometimes it's not a complete loss of memory, so victims will remember different things at different times. This very common reaction leads to accounts of the crime that may not match, which is actually a sign of veracity for those who are familiar with the complex aftermath of assault, but which is popularly (and incorrectly) regarded as a sign of fabrication and false accusation. Many people who have been raped don't recognize their assault as rape, even when it fits the legal definition.[1]

This is why sexual assault victims need someone with trauma-informed training to support them through disclosure, because taking a brain back through its original trauma without that reception and support can create deep, lasting secondary trauma. For example, imagine if someone has been in an accident and broken their leg, and it's set wrong. Reporting sexual assault can be like rebreaking and properly setting that limb. This is something a person should undertake with someone who understands different kinds of fractures, expected pain levels, and can complete the process with supportive expertise. This is not a job for someone of indifferent intentions.

Sexual assault often has a significant additional complexity: statistically, the majority of victims were attacked by someone they knew. This contradicts the common belief that sexual assaults are isolated incidents committed by strangers, and affects a victim's and a community's acceptance of the assault.

This means that victims not only need to grapple with betrayal and confusion around the assault itself, but also with betrayal and confusion around who will believe them. A victim has to reckon with not only their relationship with their attacker, but all their other relationships as well.

EFFECTS ON COMMUNITIES[2]

Sexual assault is not an isolated incident. Rape isn't just a crime against an individual—it's a crime against the community. Like individual people, many communities experience rape as a traumatic event, and, also like people, communities have a lot of emotions and reactions in the aftermath.

Many people have an image of what a rapist or abuser looks like—a trench-coated stranger in the bushes, or someone who isn't part of their community—and many people have a hard time accepting the idea that someone in their community could have committed such a crime: someone who looks like them, someone they know and trust.

This is partly because abusers groom not only their intended victims; they groom entire communities. They do this to ensure that those communities will protect them and permit their predation.

It's also because humans just love a shared feeling of safety, no matter how illusory it may be (especially for the assault victim), and learning that assault has happened in their community can make people feel helpless, afraid, and wonder whom they can trust.

Humans need community and tolerate uncertainty poorly. Ideally, a community will offer resources and support to each assault victim, both to encourage reporting, so that the community can address the crime, but also because mutual human support is what communities are about. But again, life is often not ideal.

We can see this fear and denial in how communities use the disappearing magic of passive construction to talk about sexual assault, saying "she was raped" instead of "he raped her," and framing sexual assault statistics as "rapes suffered/victims" but not as "rapes committed/rapists."

This isolates the crime and the assault victim, putting distance between them and the community, and has the effect of leaving the only witness to the crime—the victim—as the steward for the crime, with the community-given obligation to somehow make it right.

Ideally, the way to make it right involves communities supporting victims through recovering and seeking justice, but communities often define "making it right" differently. Some communities find it so hard to accept that one of their own has committed a grievous crime, or so difficult to talk about stigmatized subjects like sex, and find this renegotiation of the status quo so unacceptable that they'd rather withdraw support from the victim or blame them for the assault. For these communities, it's too hard to accept that one of their own—especially if the person is a trusted authority or well liked— could commit such a crime. They find it too hard to listen and believe. These types of community behaviors and reactions will often translate into difficulties with reporting rape.

This cultural difficulty means that when a community has to commit to the work of justice, they often view the crime as the victim's fault.

Often, a community will see the act of reporting sexual assault as a greater offense against the community than the actual assault. When this happens, often a victim reporting sexual assault is seen as an enemy: someone who's attacking the safety and sureties of that community by accusing one of their own of sexual assault.

Because of this, the community may attack the victim in several ways: withdrawing support, seeking to blame or shame the victim, telling them to forgive and forget, or trying to convince them to say nothing. The community often feels that if they can get the victim to take responsibility for addressing the assault, the community doesn't have to. They often want the incident to go away so that everything can "go back to normal."

So, even when a victim reports a crime, these communities are incentivized against pursuing justice. They may seek to invalidate or dismiss reports using a variety of reasons—by redefining rape ("Boys will be boys," "That's just normal dating activity"), by blaming the victim ("They shouldn't've been drinking while wearing that") or even, ironically, by addressing the validity of the report itself ("Why did he wait so long to report it?").

A community may even accuse a victim of making a false accusation. Stunningly, accusations of victims confabulating reports of rape are far more common than actual false report— that is, a rape victim is far more likely to be accused of falsifying a rape report than they are likely to be guilty of it. In addition, men are more likely to be raped than to be falsely accused of rape.

The Reporting Process

One of the hardest truths about this reality of community response is its potential for retraumatizing the victim.

For the victim reporting sexual assault, it's terrifying to be so vulnerable again and to share something that they may have a hard time grasping themselves. Trauma interacts deeply with memory, and it can make it hard to remember the details that reports require. Trauma often brings feelings of shame, self-blame, and worthlessness, and victims may even have fear of prosecution. (Example: if they were drinking underage, and then raped, perhaps they fear they'll get in so much trouble for drinking that they fear to report the assault.)

I cannot emphasize this enough: to understand why people don't report, it's crucial to understand the culture of the communities they live in. The community is who defines sexual assault, prosecutes offenders, and supports victims. What communities believe and teach about sexual assault will inform the beliefs and actions of assault perpetrators and victims. And perpetrators and victims *know* this.

Each of us, as individual community members, has a pretty good idea of what's acceptable and what isn't. We as communities are the ones responsible for telling those who commit and report sexual assault whether or not that's a safe thing to do. And because the majority of sexual assault is committed by someone the victim has a relationship to, it's especially crucial that we as communities offer enough support to keep victims safe so they can report their attackers.

We humans depend so much on belonging that we instinctively understand the price we may be asked to pay by communities who value some people's lives over others. And even if we've given up on belonging, we see the light sentences given to the very few rapists who even go to trial, and see the rape kits gathering dust on the shelves of evidence rooms.[3] We watch how our own people may eagerly forgive a public figure on behalf of victims in order to protect their lives from being affected by the crimes that person has committed, and maybe even eagerly attack an assault victim who dared to challenge that worldview in the first place.

Many people don't report because they are trying to protect their families. This is a common reason why children don't report the sexual assault and abuse they've suffered—they're protecting their parents from that pain, and also maybe protecting themselves from possible punishment. For some victims, reporting sexual assault can mean feeling ashamed and alone; for others, reporting can be tantamount to losing their families and friends. In some communities, it's nearly like choosing exile.

Studies have shown that if a victim can have at least one advocate—someone who believes and supports them unconditionally—then they have a far-greater chance of a faster and more complete recovery.

Reporting sexual assault is a deeply difficult process even when we as communities are doing our best to be caring and responsible. Even when people make sure to expertly support a victim through the painful process of disclosure, the victim is still undergoing a process of reliving the details of the terrible thing someone did to them, laying the details bare to strangers whose job is literally to judge, and then becoming helpless all over again as the processes of justice take over. Even in the best-case scenario, reporting can still be traumatic.

Here's my personal experience with secondary trauma: each sexual assault could be measured in terms of minutes, and each was committed by one person. Physically, I suffered each assault once, but the loss of community has been a betrayal by multiple people at a time over the course of several years.

You see, it's one thing when an abuser tells a victim that they're worthless; it's clearly harmful, especially as that outer voice of hatred becomes an inner voice of self-hatred.

But it was another thing entirely when my community's response to my reports agreed out loud with what the self-hating voices said inside. To me, that was the hardest and most-damaging part of being sexually assaulted—not each assault itself, but rather the way my community needed to reject me in order to reject the reality of what happened.

COMMON REASONS FOR NOT REPORTING

Reasons for not reporting can be countless and are unique to each survivor, but here are some common ones.

Shame and stigma

Sexual trauma and assault carry a high degree of stigma in our society; there is a lot of language around assault that characterizes those raped or assaulted as having been weak or stupid.

Guilt

Many people who are sexually assaulted blame themselves for the choices of their attackers, reasoning that if they'd done better things, or not done other things, then maybe the assault wouldn't have happened.

Denial

It can be hard to accept that something terrible has happened, and that what happened was sexual assault, even when the details fit available legal definitions.

Embarrassment

Assault creates a feeling of powerlessness, and one thing many cultures hate is lack of power. It can feel diminishing to share a moment of help-lessness, and many survivors don't report to avoid feeling additional shame, embarrassment, and powerlessness. Especially when the victim lives in a subculture that stigmatizes sex and encourages obedience/complacency/keeping things at the status quo, such potential embarrassment can feel like the threat of losing what support they do have. (Such subcultures can be family groups, friend groups, church groups, work groups, etc.)

Fear of being blamed

Many victims fear being judged, slut-shamed, or that their report will break up their family or community.

Fear of "Who will believe me?"

Communities may decide to deny the assault took place. When victims see other assault victims being openly questioned or mocked, they're understandably reluctant to expose themselves to that kind of treatment. The circumstances of the assault can also make a difference. If there is evidence of physical injuries, the person may be more likely to report. If they were intoxicated at the time and have a foggy memory of some details, they may be afraid they won't be believed.

Concerns about confidentiality

These concerns can be especially present when a victim is disclosing an assault that happened in a workplace, church, or other organization where there may be no guarantee that their personal details will remain protected.

Concerns that reporting is pointless

When victims see that untested rape kits gather dust on shelves, or know that the attacker is far more powerful and supported by the community than they are, or feel that they cannot escape their assaulter, then they may conclude that reporting is pointless.

Fear of retaliation

The majority of sexual assault is committed by someone known to the victim. The fear of retaliation may sound something like this: If they were attacked once, perhaps they can be attacked again—and what if reporting only makes the situation worse?

Financial dependence on perpetrator, who may not allow the victim to obtain help

This can be true whether the victim lives with the perpetrator or works for them. Predators tend to be very good at evaluating the vulnerability of their victims, and sexual assaults, like other patterns of abuse, tend to follow power imbalances.

Protecting a family member, friend, or partner

Many victims want to protect others, such as family members, from the life-changing reality of accepting that someone they know has been sexually assaulting their loved one.

Other victims may even want to protect their assaulter, especially if reputation, community approval, or familial safety will be changed by others knowing about the assault.

Lack of resources to obtain help— money, childcare, transportation, insurance

Getting an assault properly documented and reported can cost a victim a lot of time and money. It takes resources to visit a doctor, to have a rape kit done (some states charge victims hundreds of dollars for this), to visit law enforcement and make reports, and to participate in prosecution. If a victim cannot take time off work without endangering their employment, that is an additional barrier.

Cultural or language barriers

Reporting requires having the language to get details right, and if a victim needs an interpreter but doesn't have access to one, it can be very difficult to obtain their report. Some victims are part of communities with rape cultures, which tend to stigmatize sexual crimes and blame victims for what others have done to them.

INSTEAD OF ASKING, "Why don't people report?" maybe we can ask, "Why don't people support?"

THE DECISION TO report is complex. Reporting can be retraumatizing, empowering, or both. Part of healing is regaining a sense of control after having lost it in the assault.

Having strong support from family and friends may help. The person may also wonder whether reporting might prevent someone else from being harmed. If they think their assault is an isolated incident, they may be less likely to come forward. But if they see others reporting abuse from the same person, and see that other victims reporting are supported and protected, they may decide that coming forward is worth the risk.

1. https://journalistsresource.org/studies/government/
   criminal-justice/sexual-assault-report-why-research/
2. When I say "community," I mean our local and national
   shared communities, as well as our smaller ones—ethnic
   communities, churches, schools, organizations, etc.
3. https://www.ted.com/talks/
   kym_worthy_what_happened_when_we_tested_thousa
   nds_of_abandoned_rape_kits_in_detroit?language=en

6

VICTIM VS. SURVIVOR

"Should I use the term 'victim' or 'survivor'?" is a frequent question for those who suffer sexual assaults and for those who seek to support them.

The short answer is, "Ask the person who's been assaulted."[1]

Here's the long answer: both terms are applicable, both carry a lot of meaning for the people who are assaulted and for the people around them, and there isn't a universally accepted definition of either.

Let's talk about the different ways people define both terms, and how to choose which one you'll use in your story.

The Term Victim

Some people prefer the term "victim" because it accurately describes what their status is regarding the assault. It's also the term that makes it clear who's at fault—the perpetrator.

This is important, especially if the person who has been assaulted is part of a culture or community that downplays sexual violence, or which seeks to partly or fully blame victims for the crimes perpetrated on them by others.

It's also the descriptive term that law enforcement and the justice system use, and the term that people who are reporting assault must use for themselves, at least throughout the reporting process.

Sexual violence is an unspeakable event, but the reporting process requires the victim to speak it. Naturally, reporting can be a painfully retraumatizing event, where those reporting must relieve the details of their assault, and possibly feel helpless all over again as they submit their story to the authorities and the justice system takes over.[2]

If there's something we humans hate, it's the loss of our feeling of control. We have hatred and contempt for powerlessness because we fear it so much. Because the word "victim" implies powerlessness, it's seen by some people as synonymous with "weak," "foolish," or "dirty."

So, some people don't want to use the term "victim."

For people who feel this way about the word, "victim" is an admission of failure, a name of shame, and to attach it to oneself or to someone else is to disempower and depersonalize them.

These negative connotations to the word "victim" may increase in proportion to how much shame and stigma a given culture may attach to sexual violence. If (this kind of thinking goes), the experience was degrading, then words used to name the experience, including "victim," must be degrading as well.

It's not uncommon for people in abusive situations to prefer to identify with the abuser versus the abused. That is, it's a commonly recognized human response to prefer identifying with and supporting someone who hurts others, than to identify with someone who is helpless and hurt. Some say this is our survival instinct kicking in:

bodily helplessness feels like a kind of death, and we will do anything to survive.

It's painful to be powerless, and so some people reject or rebuke that powerlessness by rejecting the name they used while feeling powerless, and refuse to accept the term "victim." They may instead prefer the term "survivor."

Survivor

Some people prefer the term "survivor" because it makes them feel empowered and strong.

It can even carry a feeling of challenge and defiance against the perpetrator and those who supported or enabled the perpetrator's assault, and a reclaiming of one's own sense of well-being.

For them, this term can say, "I'm stronger than what happened to me." It may say, "Look how far I've come." It may say, "Respect the work I've done to survive and recover!" It's an emblem of joy and successful metamorphosis.

For others, "survivor" may be an invalidating term that they feel pressured to use by others who don't accept the painful reality of sexual assault and the recovery process.

Many people who've suffered sexual assault end up struggling with depression, anxiety, PTSD, eating disorders, substance abuse, and suicide. Recovery from sexual assault is a serious and complex endeavor that can take years, or even a lifetime, or which may never be fully resolved, especially in the case of those who complete suicide.

When people (and communities) are uncomfortable with the nature of sexual assault and recovery, they may seek to avoid accepting the truth by skipping over the pain and focusing only on the "happily ever after," that space where the person has healed from being assaulted, and now everyone around them can relax and forget the bad thing ever happened—even if that healing has not yet occurred.

Because of this denial, many assaulted people have experienced from others an expectation to be a model sexual assault survivor—someone who seems nearly superhuman, who has overcome their trauma and graduated from anguish, and can now proudly say that they aren't defined by their assault. Many of those people and communities hold the view that pain is unacceptable; only winning is welcome.

Not only using the term *victim*, but also being a victim, is to many an unacceptable state of being that opens the person to criticism and judgement from others, who may tell them that saying they were a victim of a crime is like giving up, giving their power to others, or feeling sorry for themselves.

For people who've been assaulted, and who receive this kind of pressure or judgement, the expectation to inhabit the term *survivor* can feel invalidating. Telling people that they shouldn't call themselves victims can be a rejection of who they are and the reality of whatever aftermath they're dealing with.

For them, "survivor" can mean "We don't want to hear about it" or "Get over it already, and move on." It can mean "Your pain isn't real." It may mean, "If you keep hurting or talking about the assault, we will judge you." It can mean, "You're on your own." It says to them, "That's so terrible and degrading that I can't acknowledge that reality, and you shouldn't either, and you need to pretend things are fine for my sake.

For these reasons and others, some people who have been sexually assaulted choose not to use *survivor* and instead reclaim the term *victim* as a way to reclaim the full reality of the crime committed against them.[3]

EXPERIENCES USING BOTH TERMS

I have noticed that when I speak of the rape I suffered, that when I use *victim*, I become very aware of the baggage that term carries, especially in the ears of the people hearing me speak.

I have noticed that I often anticipate that judgment toward the term *victim* and automatically seek to protect myself from that implicit rejection and blame by coupling my use of the term *victim* with examples of my strength or endurance.

Others may have different experiences with both terms, and with the support they have received or been denied as people who have suffered sexual assault and rape. All language is something that exists as a community good; that is even more true with very important words like *victim* and *survivor*.

Too often, people who suffer sexual assault or rape don't find the support they need, and may have to adjust their language in order to negotiate belonging with their audience. People speaking to a pro-survivor, anti-victim audience may use *survivor* just to negotiate safety and belonging with their audience.

A person's culture and community can have a major impact on which term they feel comfortable using.

Which Term to Use in Your Story

Making careful, honoring choices in descriptive terms can make the difference between a story that validates trauma, and a story that reenacts it.

Rape and sexual assault are, fundamentally, crimes of power. Whether the perpetrator is using a gun, alcohol, or the threat of retribution as the weapon, sexual assault is at its core an event that tells those who suffer it that they are not in control of what happens to their own body.

No matter what term a person chooses, they have undergone a deeply significant event that requires recovery. Ultimately, they are the ones who should have the power to choose. Always ask what the person who was assaulted wants to be called. If you aren't sure what to call someone who has been assaulted, then ask them.

For characters in fiction, evaluate the character's individual experience in the aftermath of sexual assault, and let them share, whether through inner or outer dialogue, what that term means to them, and why they chose it. Was it because they are in the middle of the reporting process? Is it because they want to remind the people around them that someone committed a crime against them, and that they deserve justice? Do they feel pressure to pretend that everything is fine? Do they feel judged by others? Do they feel they've recovered? There are so many reasons why a person may use a term, and may even create different terms depending on their circumstances.

Determining why a character uses *victim* or *survivor* may help you as the storyteller to define why your character chooses that term, and may also help you evaluate the possible harm that choice may do to your audience. The last thing you want a story about sexual assault to do is to make those who've been assaulted feel ashamed, unseen, or alone.

NOTE: *victim* and *victor* have the same root origin: the prefix *vict* is Latin, and means "to conquer."

1. https://www.rainn.org/articles/key-terms-and-phrases
2. https://time.com/5789032/victim-survivor-sexual-assault/
3. https://www.harpersbazaar.com/culture/features/a20138398/stop-using-survivor-to-describe-sexual-assault-victims/

7

IT CAN HAPPEN AT ANY AGE

There is a common stereotype that sexual assault and rape is an expression of passion and desire, and so that stereotype leads many to believe that sexual assault happens more to people our culture typically sees as sexually attractive, i.e. young single adults.

But sexual assault and rape is a crime that happens to every gender, race, nationality, religion, and age. Age is no protection against this crime. People assault the very old, and the very young.

Here are a few facts about sexual assault that show the types of people who are commonly sexually assaulted, proving the stereotype is incorrect.

OVER 90% of sexual assaults and rapes of children are committed by someone the child knows.

Children don't always have the emotional or cognitive capability to understand what happened to them, or the ability to express it. They also have limited independent access to resources for survival, and depend on the adults around them to believe their reports.

Since the vast majority of perpetrators are the child's family members or acquaintances, children may also fear reporting, or never get a chance. These combined factors make children very vulnerable to predation, and also adds to the underreporting of childhood sexual assaults.

PERPETRATING sexual assault and rape is not correlated with mental illness.

Statistically, assaulters are not extremely disturbed. They are "normal," people, except that they sexually assaulted or raped someone. Sexual assault is a crime, not a mental disorder.[12]

People commonly fall back on this myth for two reasons: first, because they still view rape as a crime of passion rather than a crime of power, and cannot fully understand why someone would commit a crime of sexual passion against someone they personally see as sexually undesirable whether because of age, gender, nationality, etc. A thought someone like this might have is, "I would never be attracted to that type of person, so who would want to be sexually intimate with them in any way?" This also perpetuates the myth that sexual assault is about sex or attraction; instead, we know it is about control and power.

People also believe this myth as a way to distance themselves from the perpetrators thriving in their midst. It can feel frightening to know that, in all likelihood, we are all acquainted with someone who has raped or assaulted another.

It's vital to challenge this myth of the "mentally disturbed criminal" because this belief stigmatizes the mentally ill, who are far more likely to suffer violent crime than commit it.

Most sexual assaults do not involve weapons like guns or knives. Surprise, fear, and coercion are tools that perpetrators use. These can harm anyone.

Sexual Assault of a Minor

In the United States, 1 in 10 children is a victim of sexual abuse before the age of 18. (Though this number is believed to be massively underreported, so the numbers are likely far higher.) Their dependence on adults for survival and protection, their smaller stature, and their relative lack of power, knowledge, and resources make children vulnerable to sexual assault or ongoing abuse.

Children typically are motivated to please authority figures in their life. These authority figures can include family members, teachers, or neighbors. Children are also frequently trusting and obedient, and perpetrators often abuse this by grooming children, enticing them, and winning their trust and devotion with offers of attention, affection, and gifts. Perpetrators also take advantage of the child's lack of knowledge and experience. Sometimes they reassure a victim, telling them lies such as, "Everyone does this," or saying, "I want to teach you how to do this, now that you're older."

When it comes to ensuring that young victims won't tell anyone what happened, the abuser often becomes more forceful, threatening to hurt the child or someone the child loves. Other times, the child is coerced or manipulated. The assaulter may say something like, "Think how upset your mom would be if she knew?" or, "You wouldn't want me to go to jail, would you?" Sometimes it's as violent as threatening to kill a parent or loved one.

While there are sensationalized cases where children are kidnapped or trafficked for sex, statistics show that these are by far the exceptions. Most of the time children become victims of a family member or an authority figure such as a teacher, church leader, or a trusted neighbor. (We do not mean to underplay the critical work done for those trapped in sex trafficking, but to highlight the statistical likelihood of being assaulted is higher than being trafficked.)

When writing about childhood sexual assault, don't infantilize your characters. Children are still people, just young people. They may not have the language to talk about what happened, or the tools to process how it affected them, but the assault will almost certainly have an effect on the child. They may shy away from touch, or become far too sexual for their age. They may have issues with anger or depression, and may develop health issues as their body struggles to cope with the stress. Consider that characters may have health problems such as frequent nausea, headaches, or difficulty breathing, and they (or their caretakers) may not be able to explain medically without knowledge of their trauma.

Keep in mind that for children, any act of sexual violence will be extremely traumatizing. You don't need to write about extreme circumstances to convey the pain of sexual assault. Instead, honor how painful and damaging it can be when an act of violence is a person's first introduction to sex.

SEXUAL ASSAULT OF AN ELDER

All victims have the potential of being groomed by their abuser to be more isolated and compliant, and elders are no exception.

Since rape and sexual assault are acts of violence, humiliation, and power, the assaulter does not need to be physically attracted to their victims. This is not to say that people cannot be attracted to elders, or that elders do not have active and fulfilling sex lives, but that, to a predator, sexual attraction is not the primary factor in selecting targets—vulnerability is.

What can make elders additionally vulnerable is isolation, physical weakness, and diminished mental faculties.

Isolation

Lonely people are often more vulnerable to a predator's overtures. Predators will exploit an elder who does not socialize much or have family that visits them. Many elders live alone, and others may live in a senior care facility, where the assaulter visits or works. Assaulters may feel confident that they won't get interrupted or caught.

Physical Weakness

As people age and weaken, it's easier for a perpetrator to overcome physical attempts to resist, especially in conjunction with possible isolation.

Diminished Mental Faculties

In many ways, older victims can offer assaulters the same advantages that children do. As some elders' cognitive abilities become less reliable, they may lose their ability to recognize when they are in danger. Even if they do realize what's happening, they may not have the wherewithal to control the situation.

After the assault, predators are comfortable that their victims will not report the crime. An elder may not have a reliable memory. Forgetting a sexual assault is a possibility for all sexual assault survivors (see Chapter 10), but people struggling with memory disorders are even more susceptible to this.

Even if the assault is reported, ageism may come into play and authorities may not find a victim credible. Police or social workers may question the survivor's story, citing the reliability of the victim's distorted memory, or dismissing the survivor as delusional. Even family members or friends may convince themselves that the elder is seeking attention, not understanding why anyone would rape or assault an elder.

There's also a good chance that elders will not report the crime. They may not know who they should tell. They may doubt their own memory of what happened. They may be too ashamed to share their story.

Care for Our Elders

Sexual assault is already an incredibly isolating experience—how much more painful it is for our elders, who already face a lot of isolation in our society. Please care for any elders in your story impacted by sexual assault. As with any of your characters, elders deserve peace, resolution, and justice in their story arcs.

Sexual Assault of an Adult

Obviously, the circumstances surrounding sexual assault vary widely. However, there are some common situations.

Sobriety is critical to informed consent. Many people who have been assaulted were under the influence, and sometimes predators drug their victims, thereby taking away the person's ability to respond, let alone consent. Being drugged or taken advantage of can happen to anyone: children, men, women, and genderqueer folk, and again, it is *never* the fault of the victim.

The lack of communication can also end up resulting in sexual assault. Victims may consent to some initial contact, but then want to stop. They may have a hard time expressing that to their partners due to fear or the "freeze" response, or their partners don't understand the implication of what they're told. And sometimes partners *do* know they're being asked to stop, but choose to ignore those revocations of consent. This, too, is sexual assault and rape—but many people don't realize it because so many of us still believe that coercion is accomplished only with deadly weapons, not by using drugs, alcohol, or emotional pressure.

Sometimes a person will use sexual assault to release their anger or to punish their victims. This can be the case where a victim is a current or past intimate partner of the oppressor. Once again, since rape and sexual assault are violent acts of humiliation and power, they can gratify an assaulter's need to feel as if they are in control.

Much of this book covers a variety of ways sexual assault affects adults, and I encourage readers to explore this book more thoroughly for advice on how to write about adult sexual violence. When you think about sexual assault, remember it's often not an expression of passion and desire

_____

1. https://www.ncbi.nlm.nih.gov/pmc/
   articles/PMC3777344/#:
2. https://www.psychiatrictimes.com/view/dsm-5-
   confirms-rape-crime-not-mental-disorder

8

IT'S NOT ALWAYS A MAN
ASSAULTING A WOMAN

The overwhelming trend of sexual assault in media is to show men assaulting women. This makes sense, as to the best of our knowledge, 9 out of every 10 assault survivors are women. There's no reason to stop telling those stories while that statistic remains relevant. That said, it *is* worth considering challenging that trend in stories about sexual assault, especially since assaults on men are typically underreported. For example, in military cases, 43% of female victims report as opposed to 10% of males.[1]

Assault within Queer Communities

For many Western people, violations of societal gender norms can be jarring. We're overwhelmingly socialized to equate a person's biological sex with their gender, and their gender with sexuality. The reality is, none of those things are related to one another, but society's misperception of that affects many members of the LGBTQIA+ community when it comes to sexual violence. In many ways, the very act of being queer is a long-term passive sexual assault by society. Violating gender or sexual norms can be dangerous and scary, as when you're a member of the LGBTQIA+ community, you're actively excluded from what society deems appropriate or acceptable.

Homophobia and fear of further victimization by first responders or other service providers can make it difficult for people within the queer community to report an assault. Many also fear that no one will believe them. Reporting an assault is also complicated because some do not want to be "outed" in the process of seeking help.

Remember that when writing about sexual assault in queer communities, it's nearly a guarantee your audience will have experienced some form of sexual violence, even if it's just the act of existing as a queer person in a Western society. Yes, acknowledge the trauma of those acts, but point out the beauty, love, and community that comes with Queer culture. Pride, freedom of expression, and the celebration of love of others and self all deserve recognition and portrayal in modern media. When writing about assault within queer communities, balance out the horror with the love and beauty. Keep your queer audience in mind, and understand that the act of being queer and the act of sexual assault can both be extremely isolating experiences, so emphasize the community supports that exist for queerfolk, showing your queer survivors that they're not alone, and they can seek help.

If you want to show a truly realistic portrayal of queer sexual assault, consider making the supportive aspects of the queer community the focus of your piece. Side plots and stories are important to keep a book feeling fluid and real, but finding comfort and healing can be a full-time job for many queer survivors. Honor that.

MEN ASSAULTING MEN

We can't talk about male victims of sexual assault without addressing toxic masculinity.

Toxic masculinity is not a condemnation of men or even masculinity. Rather, it's a term for the norms and expectations for men that are actively bad for men. Expressing hurt, pain, and sadness can be emasculating for men, and admitting weakness can shake a person's perception of themselves as a man. These are features of toxic masculinity that inform male responses to sexual assault.

Men assault men for the same reason anyone assaults anyone: power, control, aggression, lack of understanding, or disregard for consent. Men are affected by sexual assault in the same ways women are affected: diminished self-esteem or a poor self-image, developed mental disorders like depression, anxiety, or PTSD, as well as developed aversions to things like sex or even other men—who may remind them of their assaulters.

Sexual assault can be violent, such as forcible rape, or subtle, such as groping. Sexual assault can happen to any man, and can be equally traumatizing no matter the severity. In many ways, man-on-man sexual assault is a direct attack on the victim's sense of their own masculinity. Consider how this attack affects their self-perception: do they overcompensate, shutting down any emotions they consider weak, such as sadness or fear, by turning them into anger? Do they begin to avoid other men? Do they confront the ways the assault affected them, embrace their emotions, and actively work toward healing? Do they oversexualize themselves? Undersexualize themselves? All are valid coping mechanisms; all deserve a place in stories about sexual assault.

You don't need to portray the ideal and perfect way of healing from a sexual assault; in fact, I'd encourage you not to. Healing is messy. You can let your characters develop toxic traits, and it's more realistic if you do. But show that there is safety and healing to be found in confronting their emotions. Avoid portraying victims as weak before the assault: All men can be sexually assaulted, and all sexual assault carries the potential of being damaging. If you can, reinforce the idea that a man's distorted perception of themselves as weak after a sexual assault is just that: distorted. Let your male characters find peace, love, and closure in one form or another after a sexual assault, or at least show them taking steps on that journey.

WOMEN ASSAULTING MEN

Divulging that you were assaulted as a man is scary. When a man admits to the realities of a sexual assault, their manliness is brought into question, consciously or not. Unfortunately, expressions of vulnerability, such as crying, are still often viewed as embarrassing for a man and jarring for people observing it. As with everyone, poor reactions from friends, lovers, and families upon hearing their loved one was sexually assaulted can be retraumatizing.

Culturally speaking, we're taught that men are ready and willing to have sex all of the time. We hear this in jokes often, such as the man who's unable to turn down sex as soon as it's offered, going so far as to risk harm to themselves or their career just to get laid. Some of this has biological basis, as men in same-sex relationships tend to have more (reported) sex than women in same-sex relationships, but the oversexualization of men creates an expectation among many female assaulters that men "want it." Likewise, because of this expectation, many men don't always realize when they've been assaulted. Furthermore, those who do realize it can be hesitant to come forward for fear of losing their sense of masculinity. That expectation for men to always want sex goes both ways; being forced into sex you didn't want can disrupt your perception of yourself, resulting in thoughts like, "Why didn't I want sex?" "Why couldn't I fight her off?"

Those men who do choose to report sexual assault can receive societal backlash as those questions are levied against them. This leads to many men choosing not to disclose their sexual assault to authorities or even friends and family, as talking about it can lead to additional trauma.

When writing about men being sexually assaulted by women, it's important to consider how men are socialized in society, and how the assault disrupts that identity. Our culture's narrative about men idealizes men who are strong and in control, and when men experience violence from family or intimate partners, this cultural narrative can add to the trauma, shame, and denial a man may experience following an attack.

He may wonder, why couldn't he stop his attacker? If he could have, why didn't he? Did he not realize it was assault? If so, why not?

As with man-on-man sexual violence, it's important to be honest about the characters' struggles. The more traumatized the man is, the more attention his healing deserves in your piece. Resist brushing off woman-on-man sexual violence as as if it's not a traumatic moment. Male survivors traumatized by a woman-on-man assault will only be further traumatized by media portrayals of that assault not having an affect on a character's psyche.

WOMEN ASSAULTING WOMEN

While awareness is increasing around the sexual assault of members of the LGBTQIA+ community, "woman-to-woman rape and sexual assault globally remains largely unknown and unaddressed." Survivors of such violence often "cope alone, or with limited support, in the traumatic aftermath of their sexual victimisation."[2] This proves particularly difficult for lesbian and bisexual survivors of sexual assault, who "are among the most isolated of crime victims."[3]

One reason that this type of assault remains so statistically underreported is the legal definition of rape. In the United States, there is no unified state-level definition for rape; each state has their own unique definition.[4] As recently as 2016, laws in the UK required "penile penetration" for the assault to be legally qualified as rape.[5] The cultural construct follows: people feel like women can't (or don't) rape women.

For women who have been sexually assaulted by another woman, it can be a long road to finding someone who believes them. As with the larger queer community, research has found that "positive social support from ... gay and lesbian friends" can be particularly helpful to recovery. [6]

Remember, our humanity is not determined by our gender—our humanity is determined by our humanity.

---

1. https://www.rainn.org/statistics/criminal-justice-system
2. https://pubmed.ncbi.nlm.nih.gov/28409768/
3. *Woman-to-Woman Sexual Violence: Does She Call It Rape?* (New England Gender, Crime & Law) Paperback—February 28, 2002 by Lori B. Girshick
4. https://apps.rainn.org/policy/
5. https://www.bbc.co.uk/bbcthree/article/95769958-f129-416c-9610-c8f96504ce77
6. https://pubmed.ncbi.nlm.nih.gov/21491312/

CONSEQUENCES ON THE PSYCHE & BODY

This chapter will discuss the consequences of sexual assault on the body and psyche, as well as some commonly used tropes that downplay, flatten, or ignore those consequences. We'll discuss the psychological and physical consequences of sexual assault, and the next chapter will address the impacts on memory and trauma.

First and foremost, it's important to understand that the consequences of sexual assault vary from person to person. There is no typical psychological response to sexual assault; each reaction reflects the individual traumatic experience, with multiple sexual assaults creating further complicating trauma reactions. It's important to note that human beings react to traumatic events based on their own unique viewpoints and experiences; it's impossible to summarize the potential impact of assault in neatly bundled stereotypes. Reactions vary as much as people do.

Sexual assault is an act of power, humiliation, and violence—one that removes a sense of bodily autonomy. That loss of bodily autonomy and lack of control over the situation can cause long-term psychological effects, which in turn can have long-term physical consequences.

Physical Effects of Sexual Assault

Let's look first at the immediate aftereffects of an assault.

As with any assault, physical scars may accompany sexual assault. There may be vaginal or anal bleeding or infection, and if the perpetrator carries any STDs or diseases, they may transmit them to their victim, who will need to be tested and treated.

Some victims may also have to cope with the emotional and mental load of unplanned pregnancy. Despite what some politicians say, there's no statistical difference in the risk of pregnancy between consensual sex and rape. Those who must wrestle with this often face an additional set of choices about what do to about their pregnancy, whether that means electing to take a morning-after pill, to plan for a possible abortion, or to carry their pregnancy to term.

But beyond that, the psychological effects of sexual assault can translate into physical symptoms as well. PTSD forces the brain to produce extra cortisol: the stress hormone. This leaves the body in a constant state of tension, which can be extremely hard on the heart. It's not uncommon for people with PTSD to develop heart problems later in life.

Women who have been raped are also more likely to develop chronic pelvic pain, intense premenstrual symptoms, non-epileptic seizures, digestive problems, and arthritis.[1]

As a survivor struggles to process their trauma, they may develop coping mechanisms like substance abuse problems or eating disorders. It's very easy to pass judgment on unhealthy coping mechanisms, but it's helpful to emphasize that coping—even unhealthy coping—is good. Yes, your character may realistically develop an alcohol problem, but this isn't a moral failing; it's a way for your character to survive extremely severe psychological scars. You can also consider other dire alternatives your character might be avoiding.

These coping mechanisms can create long-term physical effects, so it's good for a person using these to seek treatment, but it's important to remember that these maladaptive coping strategies are symptoms of trauma, not a weakness of character.

PSYCHOLOGICAL EFFECTS OF SEXUAL ASSAULT

The psychological scars a person may develop exist on a spectrum, with some people noticing very little lasting effects, while others will experience life-changing emotional scars.

Shortly after a person is assaulted, they may be laughing or joking, whereas another survivor may be completely uncommunicative, and a third person may immediately feel responsible for what happened and be overwhelmed by shame.

When traumatic things happen, human bodies and brains often go into shock, and someone who's recently been assaulted may feel numb or even experience what many think of as inappropriate emotions or reactions, such as feeling like it's no big deal, or laughing about things even as they sit in an emergency room waiting for the Sexual Assault Nurse Examiner (SANE) to conduct an exam and complete a rape kit. This reaction may change either suddenly or very gradually, sometimes for no reason obvious to an external observer.

These varied reactions—shock, numbness, flashbacks, sudden mood swings—are all normal. Everyone has their own ways of processing trauma, and it's very important to nonjudgmentally support people through their own individual recovery.

When writing a traumatized character, it's important to understand the ways trauma manifests. Oftentimes people experience Acute Stress Disorder in the period immediately after the assault. This translates into people going through near-constant hypervigilance. They stop trusting people, even ones who don't deserve distrust. They may suddenly change their habits, altering their routines to avoid certain areas or situations, or stop going out altogether. Distance may develop between the survivor and their friends, family, or lovers; or, conversely, someone in the middle of recovery may become extremely attached to their supporters, often as a means of seeking safety and comfort.

At its core, sexual assault and rape is an event where someone was traumatized by being helpless or out of control. Many people may react to being sexually assaulted by trying to regain control in ways that can include exercising hypervigilance (checking locks on doors and windows, refusing to be alone) and/or accepting inappropriate victim-blaming narratives (changing what they wear).[2]

When the event is fresh, survivors might experience the time after the assault as an exceedingly long flashback, as their mind struggles to process what happened. Memories and present moments mix together. (Learn more about this in Chapter 10.) Touch may feel extremely threatening, sexual or not. Benign comments may come off as threatening, as they stay on alert for signs of imminent danger. Sleep becomes difficult, both from the inability to relax their bodies enough to sleep, and the nightmares they may experience when they do finally sleep.[3]

According to the DSM-V, if this condition lasts for longer than three months, the classification for the disorder turns into PTSD, which in acute forms looks identical to acute stress disorder.[45]

In extreme cases, such as chronic sexual abuse or sexual assault against a minor, a person may develop complex PTSD, or trauma that shapes a person's personality. At the time of writing, C-PTSD isn't recognized by the current DSM, but it is recognized by the World Health Organization. The difference between PTSD and C-PTSD is currently being debated, but the essential difference is this:

Survivors of sexual assault may develop some symptoms, all symptoms, or none at all. When writing about the psychological effects of sexual assault, it's important to remember that these moments can be extremely ugly. It's difficult watching someone have a flashback as they react entirely to a situation that's not actually happening, and if you've been assaulted, it can be absolute torture to not be sure if you're reacting to an actual threat to your safety or if you're having a flashback and perceiving the world correctly.

It's important to be honest about the realities of mental health disorders, as underselling the severity of it does a disservice to the violence of sexual assault, and the difficulties of life with a mental health disorder.[6]

Psychology is a very new form of medicine in Western societies, and receiving appropriate care can be extremely difficult or entirely inaccessible depending on a variety of factors. The lack of appropriate care can translate into unhealthy coping mechanisms. When writing about these, treat them as societal issues, not character flaws.

We cannot emphasize enough that trauma is an incredibly nuanced, variable, and individual thing. Trauma also is not static; it changes throughout the recovery process, and not always in a neatly linear fashion.

Please do your best to research trauma and to treat fictional characters who have sustained trauma as though they are real people, and take care to portray their trauma with dimensionality and care. One-dimensional portrayals of trauma help further incorrect ideas about what trauma is, and that deeply affects the experiences and available support for real sexual assault victims.

SEXUAL EFFECTS OF RAPE AND ASSAULT

Each person's recovery from rape and sexual assault is as individual as their own unique self, and that includes how assault affects a victim's sexuality.

Hypersexual behavior is about as common a reaction as hyposexual behavior. Some people feel empowered by owning their sexuality, while others feel safer avoiding sex entirely. People might feel they are unable to say no to sex, or feel like sex is fundamentally dangerous.

Please note that while a person may develop fears of certain genders, or notice a difference in sexual preference, recovery from sexual assault doesn't change a person's sexuality. For instance, bisexual people who experience sexual assault may avoid sex with the gender of their attacker, but they are still bisexual.

MAKE sure your story's response tells the real truth.

It's important to note that not every sexual assault survivor will have drawn the connection between their trauma and their behaviors. It's very common for survivors to downplay how traumatic the assault was or even forget it entirely. Dissociation is how our brains protect us from realities and experiences we're not yet equipped to handle.

If you choose to include this kind of denial-infused benign perception of an objectively horrifying event, make sure that horror is obvious to the reader, even if—or especially if—it's not obvious to your story's character. Otherwise, you as the author may run the risk of treating sexual assault like a minor plot point or a character quirk, and not as the deeply trauma-tizing experience it is. Denial is what we do to avoid trauma, but it cannot erase it.

Tropes in Fiction

We're going to talk about common sexual assault tropes in fiction, with the hope that this knowledge may help writers surpass these harmful stereotypes.

To first step to surpassing a harmful, tropey portrayal of sexual assault is to asking yourself these three key questions:

1. Why am I adding fictional sexual assault to my story?

2. Am I creating a sexual assault experience in my story for the benefit of those who've been assaulted?

3. Or am I using sexual assault as a shortcut to emotional intensity and reader sympathy?

The statistics we've shared so far make it clear that sexual assault and rape are appallingly common, and far too many people have already been harmed by this crime. When writers craft inaccurate or gratuitous portrayals of sexual assault, their stories have the potential to be not only harmful, but exploitative. Sexual assault and rape victims deserve better.

As you craft your story world, please give careful, searching, and honest thought to why you will add fictional sexual assault to the real-world tally. Getting this right has the power to help the hurting; misrepresentation has the potential for real-world harm.

Now that you know about some of the psychological and physical impacts of sexual assault, let's look at the common tropes in fiction that undermine and ignore those impacts. It's important to note that while many of these tropes typically fall on womxn in any given story, the same general principles apply across genders.

Disposable Women & Fridging

There's a common trope in the media where a female love interest is sexually assaulted, only to be rescued by the male protagonist. Often time this trope uses sexual violence as a way to emphasize the heroism of the hero, never really acknowledging the short- and long-term harm sexual assaults can cause to the female character. When writing about sexual assault, it's important to acknowledge the scars it causes in an accurate way. Sexual assault isn't pretty, and the scars it leaves can be lifelong. Don't use sexual assault as a tool to uplift a male protagonist's heroism or to develop his character.[789]

Rape as a Shortcut

A secondary trope is the idea that the "worst thing that could happen" to a female character is that she be raped. While it's absolutely true that rape is horrific, the idea that having a character be raped is a shortcut to narrative or character depth is a tired one.[10] Particularly if you are writing horror, be very careful when you introduce rape as a plot element. If you're writing in an imagined or alternate world and you choose to include sexual violence, ask yourself why. You could choose to create a world without sexual violence, so what are your reasons for including it?

Rape is regularly shown as a shortcut for why a character might be depressed, or as a shortcut for any substantive backstory at all. [11][12] Rape is sometimes used as the only motivator for a "strong female character," segueing neatly into rape-revenge films like *Kill Bill*.[13] This isn't to say that rape can't be included in a story, or that sexual assault can't be part of a character's backstory, but that it needs to be done with great intentionality.

Broken Bird

These (usually female-coded) characters are completely broken after an assault. They lose faith and hope in everything, become emotionally absent, and refuse to engage with things that once brought them joy. Their troubled past, which often includes sexual assault, is kept a secret, and is often used as a big reveal.

This trope is problematic because of its pervasive nature and the flattening of the survivor's experience. This sort of reaction can be absolutely realistic, but it leads to the perception that if someone isn't completely broken/emotionally absent/an empty shell after their sexual assault, they must be lying about it, exaggerating, or some other victim-blaming false logic.[14]

THERE ARE entire pages dedicated to sexual harassment and rape tropes that you can explore at your leisure, but remember, if you choose to include rape or other sexual assault in your manuscript, proceed with intent and caution.[15][16]

1. https://www.verywellmind.com/symptoms-of-ptsd-after-a-rape-2797203
2. https://www.brit.co/what-ptsd-looks-like-for-sexual-assault-survivors/
3. https://www.verywellmind.com/symptoms-of-ptsd-after-a-rape-2797203
4. https://digitalrepository.unm.edu/psy_etds/172/
5. https://www.mayoclinic.org/diseases-conditions/post-traumatic-stress-disorder/symptoms-causes/syc-20355967
6. https://www.verywellmind.com/what-is-complex-ptsd-2797491
7. https://tvtropes.org/pmwiki/pmwiki.php/Main/DisposableWoman

8. https://tvtropes.org/pmwiki/pmwiki.php/
   Main/StuffedIntoTheFridge
9.
10. https://apex-magazine.com/writing-about-rape/
11. https://www.jstor.org/stable/41158073
12. https://tvtropes.org/pmwiki/pmwiki.php/
    Main/RapeAsBackstory
13. https://www.glamour.com/story/keira-knightley-on-
    rape-backstory-in-movies-tv-shows
14. https://tvtropes.org/pmwiki/pmwiki.php/
    Main/BrokenBird
15. https://tvtropes.org/pmwiki/pmwiki.php/
    Main/SexualHarassmentAndRapeTropes
16. https://mythcreants.com/blog/six-rape-tropes-and-
    how-to-replace-them/

10

MEMORY AND TRAUMA AROUND SEXUAL ASSAULT

In most people's minds, trauma comes in the form of flashbacks, agonizing sepia scenes where the characters reimagine everything that happened to them in crisp detail. We see this in books like *Sharp Objects* by Gillian Flynn and shows like *Law and Order: SVU*. These are convenient storytelling ways to reveal the past in fragments, increasing the tension.

In real life, however, when it comes to sexual assault, that isn't always the case. Survivors can miss details, get their stories mixed up, and occasionally suffer from complete amnesia. This is because when enduring trauma, our memories are input differently than typical everyday memories.

In "Why Sexual Assault Survivors Forget the Details," Linda Geddes explains that, "Usually we encode what we see, hear, smell, taste and physically sense, as well as how that all slots together and what it means to us—and together, those different types of information enable us to recall events as a coherent story. But during traumatic events, our bodies are flooded with stress hormones. These encourage the brain to focus on the here and now, at the expense of the bigger picture."[1]

That doesn't mean that every time we experience trauma our brain is scrambled, but it does mean a character who has experienced sexual assault most likely won't remember every detail like a vivid movie. And when it comes to survivors of childhood sexual abuse, the memories get even trickier.[2]

In fact, in Dr. Bessel Van Der Kolk's *The Body Keeps the Score: Brain, Mind, and Body in the Healing of Trauma*, Kolk found complete memory loss after childhood sexual abuse happened with around 19% to 38% of people. It's a standard coping mechanism our body applies when we aren't strong enough to handle what's being thrown at us. With those statistics, it's easy to think you can use sexual assault as a plot device without acknowledging the symptoms of the trauma if the character has amnesia. After all, they don't remember, so it shouldn't affect them, right?

That isn't the case. While the mind may not have a tangible memory, the body remembers. According to Melissa and Joshua Hall, "Child-hood sexual abuse has been correlated with higher levels of depression, guilt, shame, self-blame, eating disorders, somatic concerns, anxiety, dissociative patterns, repression, denial, sexual problems, and relationship problems."[3] Even without the memories, these issues can follow assault survivors through their lives. While everyone presents differently, a character who has experienced childhood sexual abuse mostly likely has body issues, anxiety, significant relationship trouble, and either hypersexuality or sex repulsion. Even if they are healing during the novel, it's important to acknowledge the work they have done to get there and the possible issues they are working through.

A great example of this is the young adult novel *The Perks of Being a Wallflower* by Stephen Chbosky. The main character, Charlie, spends most of the novel dealing with depression, feel-ings of isolation, anxiety, and panic attacks. At first, Charlie believes his depression stems from the death of his best friend and his favorite aunt.

However, as the story progresses, the more poignant aspects of his PTSD arrive, and he learns he was sexually abused as a child by his aunt Helen. He begins to have more frequent flashbacks of his aunt, not abusing him but just being around him. This leads to his first sexual encounter, which makes him uncomfortable, and eventually ends with him finally remembering the abuse. Through this novel, we can see how sexual abuse has affected Charlie, even though he doesn't remember it at first. He is depressed, anxious, socially inept, and uncomfortable in intimate situations. It shows the reader that symptoms of sexual abuse don't rely on memory to take hold.[4]

We see the same thing in the adult horror novel *Gerald's Game* by Stephen King (also referenced in Chapter 4). In this novel, Jessie finds herself handcuffed to a bed in the middle of nowhere with her husband, dead from a stroke, on the floor. With no one coming for them, Jessie begins to hallucinate and eventually remembers his repressed sexual assault. The novel ends with her escape—not only from the bed, but from her repression. She acknowledges the truth and writes her story, deciding to not let angry men control her life ever again. While there are not a lot of flashbacks about her adult life in this novel, we see the impact of Jessie's assault from how she interacts with her husband. He is controlling and aggressive, and when Jessie initially says she doesn't want to be handcuffed, he disregards her, and she becomes submissive. Here we see how her assault led her to enter into an unhealthy relationship. We see more impacts of her assault through her hallucinations. She sees different versions of herself and her husband. They mock her, calling her an idiot, crazy, and helpless. Knowing that they are figments of Jessie's imagination, we see how her assault made her feel about herself.[5]

Both novels are incredibly different, and the characters' reactions to their assaults present differently, but they both represent works that showcase the consequences of sexual abuse regardless of memory.

While your character doesn't have to have amnesia paired with an epiphany, it is uncommon for sexual assault survivors to remember everything. For better realism, focus not on the act itself, but what came after. Dig into your character, their personality, and how they would react. Look into the common symptoms of assault, and find which symptoms make sense for your character.

The most important thing I learned about sexual assault and memory is that you do not have to remember the assault to be a valid survivor, and you do not need to remember the assault in order to heal.[6] While television loves to play with the recovering-memories trope, it's not necessary for healing and may even prove to be unhelpful. Narratives like this encourage people to re-experience their trauma and typically ignore a valid healing process in favor of shocking their audience. This is entirely unhelpful to survivors who may read your work, as focusing on therapy and healing is more important than recalling the event itself. And you don't want young survivors to attempt to force themselves to go places mentally that will be harmful.[78]

Overall, when writing a character who has experienced sexual assault, it's important not to police their memories. Don't force a storyline where your character remembers every gritty detail if the details aren't relevant to the plot. Don't write that the character's abuse isn't real if they don't remember it. Don't harp on remembering and forget healing, and don't make a character a survivor (make them experience sexual abuse) if you're not going to give them something to survive (have no problems after abuse is over).[9]

---

1. https://healinghonestly.com/memory/why-we-can%E2%80%99t-remember
2. https://healinghonestly.com/memory/what-its-remember-what-you-cant-remember
3. https://www.sciencedirect.com/science/article/abs/pii/014521349090099F
4. https://www.ccasa.org/survivorhood-portrayed/
5. https://netflakes.ca/2018/02/12/geralds-game-me-too-horror-podcast/
6. https://istss.org/public-resources/what-is-childhood-trauma/remembering-childhood-trauma
7. https://istss.org/public-resources/what-is-childhood-trauma/remembering-childhood-trauma
8. https://www.counseling.org/docs/disaster-and-trauma_sexual-abuse/long-term-effects-of-childhood-sexual-abuse.pdf?sfvrsn=2
9. https://www.bbc.com/future/article/20180926-myths-about-sexual-assault-and-rape-debunked

TAKE A BREATH

Y ou've finished the book! Thank you for being willing to learn so much about a complex topic. We hope that what you've learned in this Guide will help you approach yourself, others, and your characters with more compassion, clarity, and intent.

As we mentioned at the beginning of the Guide, as you read, you may have felt uncomfortable in spots, and you may have realized that you, too, are a survivor.

So what do you do if you realize you've been assaulted?

What do you do if you realize that you or someone you love has assaulted someone?

First, take a deep breath. It's a hard thing to realize, and can sometimes make you look at the world and the people you love (or who love you) in a different way.

We highly recommend RAINN's sexual assault telephone hotline: 1.800.656.HOPE (4673). We also encourage you to seek out the help of a qualified therapist.[1]

Most of all, be kind to yourself. Take a breath. You matter, and so do your stories.

---

1. https://www.rainn.org/articles/how-can-therapy-help

#WRITEDIVERSITYRIGHT PLEDGE

Join us on social media with your #WriteDiversityRight pledge. Tag us in your post—we want to hear from you!

I pledge to do my absolute best, do my due diligence, hire a sensitivity reader(s), and listen to and boost autistic voices.

As a reminder, please remember to include content warnings when submitting materials to agents, editors, etc. Remember that they're human beings with their vast array of lived experiences and could be vulnerable in ways you might not be aware of.

AFTERWORD

Thank you for reading our Incomplete Guide! We hope you found it helpful. Please leave a review so that other people can find it.

You heard from many of our editors and readers in this book, and you've gotten a taste of what sort of people they are: kind, thoughtful, wise, and really, really cool. And best of all? They love stories.

Check out our wide array of readers at www.saltandsagebooks.com. Tell us that you came through the Incomplete Guide for a 10% discount.

You can find us on Twitter, Instagram, and Facebook—just search "Salt and Sage Books."

If you are an autistic creator and would like to contribute to a future, expanded version, we want to hear from you! Reach out to hello@saltandsagebooks.com and use the subject "INCOMPLETE".

ADDITIONAL RESOURCES: BOOKS

Support your local bookstores and find these #ownvoices books here: https://bookshop.org/lists/metoo-books

———

Fiction:

The Nowhere Girls by Amy Lynn Reed

Speak by Laurie Halse Anderson

Break the Fall by Jennifer Iacopelli

The Music of What Happens by Bill Konigsberg

Girl Made of Stars by Ashley Herring BLake

Exit, Pursued By A Bear by E. K. Johnston

Moxie by Jennifer Mathieu

The Way I Used to Be by Amber Smith

Dreadnought by April Daniels

Kaleidoscope Song by Fox Benwell

What I Leave Behind by Alison McGhee

All the Rage by Courtney Summers

What We Saw by Aaron Hartzler

Saints and Misfits by S. K. Ali

Asking for It by Louise O'Neill

Some Boys by Patty Blount

Sold by Patricia McCormick

What Happens Next by Colleen Clayton

A Girl Like That by Tanaz Bhathena

Blood, Water, Paint by Joy McCullough

Dreamland by Sarah Dessen

Symptoms of Being Human by Jeff Garvin

Crossing the Tracks by Barbara Stuber

I Hadn't Meant to Tell You This by Jacqueline Woodson

Trail of Crumbs by Lisa J. Lawrence

Good and Gone by Megan Frazer Blakemore

Honor Code by Kiersi Burkhart

Learning to Breathe by Janice Lynn Mather

The Opposite of Innocent by Sonya Sones

Milk and Honey by Rupi Kaur

Nonfiction & Memoirs

We Should All Be Feminists by Chimamanda Ngozi Adichie

Asking For It: The Alarming Rise of Rape Culture—and What We Can Do About It by Kate Harding

Not That Bad by Roxane Gay

Women of Resistance

Things We Haven't Said edited by Erin Moulton

I Have the Right To by Chessy Prout

No More Excuses: Dismantling Rape Culture by Amber J. Keyser

Yes means Yes!: Visions of Female Sexual Power and a World Without Rape by Jaclyn Friedman and Jessica Valenti

Shout by Laurie Halse Anderson

Ask: Building Consent Culture by Kitty Stryker

Consent on Campus by Donna Freitas

Written on the Body by Lexie Bean, Dean Spade, Nyala Moon

C is for Consent by Eleanor Morrison (board book)

What Does Consent Really Mean? by Pete Wallis

ADDITIONAL RESOURCES: WEBSITES

#WhyIDidntReport

https://www.ted.com/
playlists/582/the_conversation_around_sexual_
assault

https://www.ted.com/
talks/jessica_ladd_the_reporting_system_that_s
exual_assault_survivors_want

https://www.sanfordjournal.org/sjpp/2018/
10/2/we-believe-women

https://wrappedupinbooks.org/readers-
advisory-resources/booklist-sexual-assault-rape-
and-dating-violence-in-ya-novels/

https://www.nytimes.com/2018/09/12/books/
me-too-young-adult-fiction.html

https://www.npr.org/2016/04/01/472584700/
when-it-comes-to-talking-sex-young-adult-
books-can-be-a-parents-best-friend

http://www.middlebury.edu/media/view/
240971/authentic/sable_article.pdf

This study revealed that only 18% of adult
women's rapes and 11% of the assaults on children were reported. (https://pubmed.ncbi.nlm.
nih.gov/7298584/)

Cases of sexual assault on men (MSA) are even
more underreported and unaddressed. (https://
www.ncbi.nlm.nih.gov/pmc/
articles/PMC6085940/)

Sexually assaulted children: national estimates
and characteristics https://www.ncjrs.gov/pdf-
files1/ojjdp/214383.pdf

Why women don't report sexual assault:
https://pubmed.ncbi.nlm.nih.gov/7298584/

The complex reasons sexual assaults go unreported: https://www.wsj.com/articles/the-
complex-reasons-sexual-assaults-go-unreported-
1538227801

Why we're still asking why survivors don't report
sexual assault—and how we can change:
https://www.marketwatch.com/story/why-

were-still-asking-why-survivors-dont-report-
sexual-assault——and-how-we-can-change-
2018-09-27

Why many sexual assault survivors may not
come forward for years: https://journalistsre-
source.org/studies/government/criminal-
justice/sexual-assault-report-why-research/

Two Helpful Analogies

https://www.youtube.com/watch?
v=pZwvrxVavnQ

https://feministphilosophers.wordpress.com/
2011/09/17/a-useful-rape-analogy/

ABOUT THE AUTHOR

Salt and Sage Books is an editing company centered on the idea that a rising tide lifts all boats.

We are a creative community of devoted readers, writers, and editors, hailing from the desert's sunwashed sage to the coast's shining seas, and we've brought together our diverse skills and experiences in a single welcoming place, to help writers like you.

When you choose Salt and Sage, you join a creative community working together to change the world through story.

Check out our Incomplete Guides series for an accessible first step into writing diversely.

You'll find a wide range of editors, sensitivity and expert readers, and beta readers on our website, www.saltandsagebooks.com.

Welcome to the rising tide.

How to Write Atheist Characters

How to Write Intersex Characters

How to Write Latinx Characters

How to Write Queer Characters

How to Write Characters from the U.K.

How to Write Characters from Spain

How to Write about Anxiety

How to Write about PTSD and Trauma

How to Write about Therapy

And more!

If you'd like to see one of these guides sooner than another or have ideas for another guide, please email us at hello@saltandsagebooks.com.

Made in the USA
Las Vegas, NV
10 July 2021

26225821R00085